DATE			

53x 2-01 7-01 LJ

PICTURE LIBRARY

BIG CATS

PICTURE LIBRARY

BIG CATS

N.S. Barrett

Franklin Watts

London   New York   Sydney   Toronto

© 1988 Franklin Watts Ltd

First published in Great Britain
    1988 by
Franklin Watts Ltd
12a Golden Square
London W1R 4BA

First published in the USA by
Franklin Watts Inc
387 Park Avenue South
New York
N.Y. 10016

First published in Australia by
Franklin Watts
14 Mars Road
Lane Cove
2066 NSW

UK ISBN: 0 86313 640 0
US ISBN: 0-531-10527-X
Library of Congress Catalog Card
Number 87-50847

Printed in Italy

Designed by
Barrett & Willard

Photographs by
Survival Anglia
Pat Morris
ZEFA
N.S. Barrett Collection

Illustrations by
Rhoda & Robert Burns

Technical Consultant
Michael Chinery

Contents

Introduction

Cats are among the most graceful creatures in the animal kingdom. The big cats of the wild, such as lions, tigers and leopards, can be fierce animals. But they have much in common with domestic cats.

They move in the same elegant and sometimes stealthy way. They are carnivores, or meat-eaters, stalking their prey and then pouncing on it. They hunt mainly at night, and have keen hearing.

△ A group of male lions enjoy a meal. The lionesses, who do most of the hunting, will have their share next, and the cubs get what is left.

Big cats live in many parts of the world, mainly in warm lands. Lions live in Africa and a small area of India, while tigers are to be found in many parts of Asia. Africa and Asia are the home of the leopard and cheetah, too. The jaguar and puma live in the Americas.

Lions live and hunt in social groups called prides. Most of the other cats are solitary animals, and roam large areas by themselves.

△ A tiger relaxes in the shade of the forest, washing itself lazily just like a domestic cat.

Looking at big cats

Eyes in the light . . .

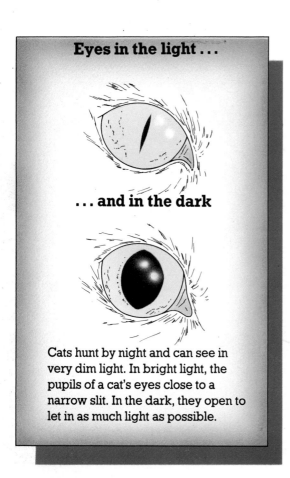

. . . and in the dark

Cats hunt by night and can see in very dim light. In bright light, the pupils of a cat's eyes close to a narrow slit. In the dark, they open to let in as much light as possible.

Cats around the world

Bigs cats live in most parts of the world, but not in Australia or the polar regions.

 Leopard

 Jaguar

 Lion

 Cheetah

 Puma

Tiger

Sheathed claws

Cats, except for cheetahs, retract (draw in) their claws when not using them. This protects the claws when the cats are running, for example. The claws remain sharp and ready for use when needed.

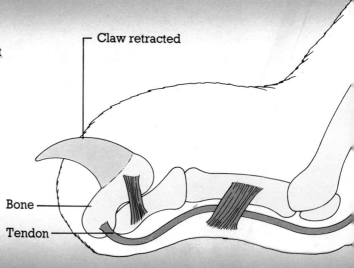

Claw retracted

Bone

Tendon

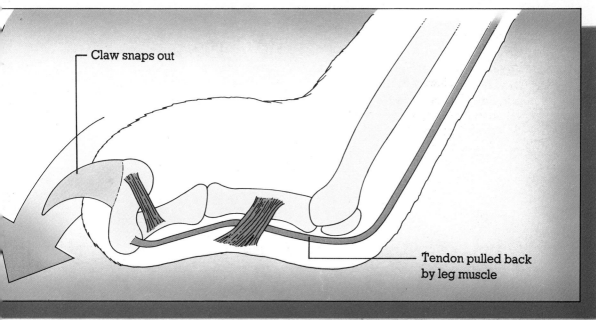

Claw snaps out

Tendon pulled back
by leg muscle

Lions

The lion is known as the "king of beasts." It is feared by most other animals, and its roar can be heard 8 km (5 miles) away. The lionesses do most of the hunting, while the lions guard against enemies.

Most lions live in Africa, on the grassy plains. Their main source of food is provided by the great herds of grazing animals, such as zebra and various kinds of antelope. But they eat anything they can catch.

▽ A lone lioness stands amid springbok and vultures on open scrubland. Most animals that lions enjoy eating can run faster than lions. So lions hunt in groups. They may chase their prey toward other lions hidden in long grass, or perhaps pick off a weak or sick animal.

Most prides consist of 10 to 20 members, although they can be as large as 35. A pride has from one to three adult males, and the rest are lionesses and cubs.

Young males are forced out of the pride at two or three years old. They might have to join up with other males in order to catch enough prey to survive. They eventually join another pride.

△ A group of lions at a watering place. Lions can go for several days without eating, but they must drink regularly.

▷ A pride of lions at sunrise. Lions live together peacefully. The lionesses care for their cubs, which are very lively and enjoy playing games together.

Lions spend as much as 20 hours a day sleeping or resting. They do much of their hunting at night, and sometimes travel up to 24 km (15 miles) in search of prey. After a big meal they may rest for 24 hours.

While the lionesses do the hunting, the adult males defend the rest of the pride against their enemies, such as hyenas who might try to take the cubs.

◁ A five-week-old lion cub ventures out by itself.

▷ A lioness stretches out in the branches of a tree for a shady rest.

▽ Just like a domestic cat with kittens, the lioness carries her cubs in her mouth one at a time.

Tigers

Tigers live in parts of Asia. Their habitats range from the hot jungles of Malaysia to the dry thorn woods of India. Some live in the snowy forests of Siberia.

Tigers hunt alone, usually at night. They prefer large prey, such as deer and wild pigs, but they will eat smaller animals, such as monkeys and frogs. They particularly like porcupines, but sometimes hurt themselves on the sharp quills.

▽ A tiger bounds through the forest, charging after prey. Tigers are fast over short distances and can leap 6 m (20 ft). But they cannot chase their prey for very long, because they soon tire.

The stripes of the tiger help it to hide from its prey. As it prowls through long grass or the light and shade of the jungle, it blends in with its surroundings.

Adult male tigers, like other male cats, claim a territory by marking out an area with body fluids. The scent warns other males to keep out. But a male may share his territory with one or more females.

△ Tigers are good swimmers and enjoy a dip to cool off on a hot day. Although they live alone, they are not always unfriendly when they meet other tigers, and sometimes share a kill.

All tigers belong to the same species, but their color and size vary slightly, depending on where they come from. The farther north tigers live, the bigger they are. The majestic Siberian tiger (left) is the biggest of all.

Siberian tigers also have paler coats. But the white tigers (above and right) are freaks of nature, not separate species.

Spotted cats

Several of the big cats are noted for their spots. The leopard and the jaguar are similar animals. They are both good swimmers and climbers, and often lie along a branch, basking in the sun.

The spots of leopards and jaguars form rosettes. The rosettes on a jaguar's coat have central spots. The ounce, or snow leopard, has a paler and thicker coat. The smaller ocelot has thick black spots.

▽ The leopard is a powerful cat. It feeds on all kinds of prey, including antelope, young baboons and monkeys, birds, snakes and fish. It often drags large prey up into a tree to keep it safe from hyenas and jackals.

Cheetahs are the fastest of all land animals. Unlike most other big cats, they hunt during the day. They live in open country, alone, in pairs or sometimes in family groups.

Their body structure is different from that of the other big cats. They have long, slender legs and a small head on high shoulders. Their coats are covered with round, dark spots.

△ Cheetahs often perch on a hillock or mound looking for prey. They have excellent eyesight and can see long distances.

△ The jaguar is the biggest cat in the Americas. It ranges from the southwestern United States, through Central and South America and Argentina.

◁ The ocelot is a smaller cat that lives in much the same areas as the jaguar.

▷ A leopard (top) keeps her cubs in the hollow of a tree or a cave. A cheetah cub (below left) and a baby serval (below right). The serval is a smaller cat from Africa.

△ Snow leopard cubs in a zoo. The snow leopard, or ounce, lives in the Himalayas and other mountain ranges of central Asia. It has a thick, warm coat, and its coloring blends with its rocky, snowy habitat.

▷ The black panther is a true leopard. The only difference is that the coat is so dark that its spots can scarcely be seen.

Other cats

◁ The mountain lion is also called a cougar or a puma. Some of these cats are as big as leopards. They are found in many parts of North and South America, particularly in wooded, mountainous areas.

▽ Mountain lions like areas with steep cliffs or canyons. They usually hunt during the night, and their chief prey is deer. They have a blood-curdling cry, but they are generally timid toward people.

There are several types of lynxes. They differ from the true cats, having short tails, side-whiskers and hairy ear tufts. They live on small animals such as rabbits.

◁ The European lynx lives in mountain forests.

▽ Bobcats, which are closely related to the Canadian lynx, are found in wooded areas in North America.

△ The caracal lynx comes from Africa and southwestern Asia. It lives on many kinds of prey, from mice to small antelopes, including birds, reptiles and domestic animals.

▷ The jaguarundi is a strange-looking spotted cat with short legs and a long body. Jaguarundis range from the southern United States to South America. Their coats vary from almost black to reddish yellow.

The story of big cats

The cat family
In the animal kingdom, animals that eat flesh are grouped in the order Carnivora. Cats make up a family within this order, called Felidae.

Saber toothed tigers
The cat family began to appear about 35 million years ago. It developed along two main lines, the cats we know today and the saber tooths. The saber tooth cats, which attacked their prey with huge fangs, died out a few thousand years ago.

△ Fossil remains of the skull of a saber toothed cat found in California.

King of beasts
For thousands of years, people have looked upon the male lion as the "king of beasts." With its majestic mane and terrifying roar, it became a symbol of power. The tiger, too, was regarded as a most ferocious animal.

△ Like the ancient Romans, the Mogul rulers of India enjoyed watching fights between men and beasts.

Hunting big cats
Because of their reputation, these big cats became a challenge, and people began to hunt them for sport. It was looked upon as a brave thing to do, showing great courage.

Over 3,000 years ago, the Egyptian pharaoh Amenhotep III hunted lions with bow and arrows from a chariot, and killed over a hundred in this way. Some 300 years ago, the Mogul emperors of India used spears to hunt lions. Lions and tigers have been hunted on horseback and from elephants, and the introduction of the rifle made killing them much easier.

△ The riders seem in more danger than the tiger in this painting of a tiger hunt in India in the 1890s.

Big cats in captivity

We also began to tame big cats thousands of years ago. Lions were tamed and bred by some of the rulers of ancient Egypt and Assyria. The Roman emperor Heliogabalus rode in a chariot pulled by lions. In India, for hundreds of years the cheetah has been trained for hunting antelope and other game.

The ancient Romans used lions and other wild animals in their outdoor entertainments, called circuses. Armed men called gladiators sometimes fought against lions, and condemned criminals and Christians were sometimes thrown to the lions. Mogul rulers of India were entertained by battles between men and lions or tigers.

In modern circuses, lions are trained to do tricks. They are popular animals in zoos and safari parks, too, as are the other big cats.

△ Cheetahs have been trained and used for hunting for hundreds of years.

Survival

The survival of some kinds of big cats today is seriously threatened. The destruction of the places where they live, their natural habitats, has reduced their numbers considerably. The hunting of big cats for sport and for their skins to make furs is another threat to their survival.

The big cats in danger include the tiger, jaguar, cheetah, snow leopard, ocelot, mountain lion, and clouded leopard. Despite conservation programs and protection laws, these animals are still being hunted and shot.

Facts and records

Fastest

The cheetah is the fastest of the big cats. Its speed over short distances has been measured at about 100 km/h (62 mph), faster than any other animal, even the swiftest antelope.

△ The cheetah can run faster for short distances than any other animal.

Oldest

Big cats do not usually live for more than 15 years in the wild. The greatest recorded age for a big cat in captivity is 29 years, for a lion that died about 80 years ago in a German zoo.

Heaviest

Weights of over 325 kg (715 lb) have been reported by hunters for Siberian tigers, but it is not known how reliable their claims are. In captivity, a lion reared from a cub reached a weight of 375 kg (826 lb), twice the average of an adult male in the wild.

Cubs

The cubs of big cats are blind and helpless at birth. But their eyes open after a few days.

△ A 2-day-old leopard cub. Cubs are blind for the first few days of their lives.

Asiatic lions

Lions used to live in central and northern India, Iran and the Arabian peninsula. By 1900, however, all had disappeared except for a few in the Gir Forest, in northwestern India. This small area was made into a wildlife sanctuary, where two or three hundred Asiatic lions live and breed today.

△ An Asiatic lion in the Gir Sanctuary in India.

Glossary

Caracal
A type of lynx.

Carnivore
An animal that eats meat, or flesh.

Conservation
The practice of protecting wild animals in their natural habitats.

Cougar
Another name for the puma or mountain lion, used particularly in Florida.

Extinct
No longer existing. Many types of big cats are in danger of dying out, or becoming extinct.

Felidae
The scientific name for the cat family.

Fossil
Ancient bones or other remains of animals preserved over the years.

Habitat
The natural abode of an animal in the wild.

Jaguarundi
A smaller cat of the Americas that, despite its name, has no

particular connection with the jaguar.

Ounce
Another name for the snow leopard.

Panther
Another name for the leopard. A black panther is a leopard with a dark coat.

Prey
An animal hunted for food.

Pride
A group of lions that live together.

Saber toothed tiger
An extinct type of cat. The various saber tooth cats died out some thousands of years ago.

Sanctuary
A protected animal reserve, often open to visitors and tourists.

Solitary
A solitary animal is one that normally lives and hunts alone.

Species
A particular kind of animal. The members of a species are alike and the males and females can breed with each other.

Index